More Praise for YOU CAN HAVE IT ALL

"Heil bends languages and time to create
a space between spaces."

Giuliana Kiersz

"In her debut poetry collection, Kathleen Heil unleashes a
poetic kinesis teeming with sophisticated splendour. *You Can
Have It All* gives shape to 'curious, furious beauty,' gifting us
poems determined to 'sit inside the yet.' This book is bright
with becoming."

Geffrey Davis

Praise for Kathleen's Literary Translations

"Heil's translations are themselves works of the highest literary
refinement and ingenuity."

Wayne Kostenbaum

"What an ingenious way of translating ... a true delight ... Such a
gift proves true throughout this all-in-all inventive rendering."

Mary Ann Caws

"Heil translates ... with a sensitivity to the differences between the
way the two languages convey distinctions of meaning."

Daniel Barbiero, *Arteidolia*

"Heil has deftly captured the nimble verve ... of the originals."

Sylee Gore, *Harriet Books*

Kathleen Heil

YOU CAN HAVE IT ALL

MOIST

First published in 2024 by MOIST
https://www.moistbooks.com

ISBN: 978-1-913430-18-4

Cover image © Nastassja Simensky 2024

A catalogue record for this book is available from the British Library.

YOU CAN

HAVE IT

ALL

YOU CAN

manifold theory

The year I went home with less luck and no clothes
I thought often about the Book of Job.

Everybody was angry about the boundary limits;
we got down on our knees we came we screamed.

To lend meaning to stochastic walks, smack the fly
buzzing about your storm drained heart. Beneath

the surface tension, a parabolic arc (lies)
we reserved the spot at the top in advance

so pretty so proud so petty so there. There
but for now there and there a bomb a bomb

goes off. Our fists punch up the ceiling (wrong)
oh why oh why oh why

Collection & Identification

unexploded:

On average, Germany's *Kampfmittelbeseitigungsdienst* deactivates a
bomb every two weeks. An occurrence that crops up with every
new building built. Every Rome roamed. The crows pick at trash
on the dais of the Holocaust memorial.

> In German, reported speech is indicated via
> the use of what is known as the *Konjunktiv I.*
> Culler sagte, vielleicht sei Literatur wie ein Unkraut.

ordinance:

Last week in Berlin, another bomb to be dismantled.
We were all moaning, the S-Bahn colicky,
my translation for the trains when *unregelmäßig.*
My friend from Donetsk showed me a photo on his phone
of an axe mounted on a wall with a feather tied to it.
We are trying to escape,

> he said. The axe hung
> over his head.

unexploded:

For the quincentennial celebration of the Reformation, Lego
made a Martin Luther, but they couldn't justify changing the
machinery for just one man.

> He is all constituent parts.
> Harry Potter hair,

a Darth Vader body, the torso
a nameless knight from the castle
collection.

unexploded:

The first message over the internet was host to host. When
she left the convent, there was no explanation,

> just a prayer and visitations. When asked, what's next,
> she said, "I'll lie in the foetal position
> and watch Netflix."
> He slapped her with packing tape for the journey
> home. "Fragile," it said. The author attributed
> the dire results, in part, to an "existential
> conflict."

Harvey Wallbanger

An itinerant preacher punched me
          in the face. See, I'd asked him; to
see what suffering felt like. We were not

on my yacht, not in my shanty, we were
          playing a round of bocce, deciding
whose turn it was, tuning our attention

to the impact of stone on stone.
          I'm the ball, you say.
I'm the ball? Modifying

the field is like modifying the field.
          Best done on a riding mower, so
you don't have to feel the effort behind

the blades but for a pleasant rocking
          buzz. We drained our drinks,
opening our umbrellas, in wait:

Love Letter To David Wojnarowicz

"Where we want to go is back to beauty." We want to go back to the idiosyncrasy of clouds amid the world's fury. My world got so small. You pushed it open threw your fury into splendour. <u>Not letting anyone forget splendour doesn't make fury less legitimate.</u> It's not as if you died young by accident. The creatures charging off a cliff are charging their splendour provoked by a push. Systemic failures are involved. Husch, husch.

The sun is shining today, unrepentant. Yesterday I went to the doctor after meaning to go for months. I was ashamed to show her my pain. Ashamed I had waited so long. Afraid of a push where care would lie, having known doctors who'd call a stone a cloud, then laugh. Then you're left alone to deal with the stone, ha ha. It might send you careening into an abyss, but don't think us stupid for sprinting. We know more than you think, even when our mouths are stitched shut, even when it seems we're the ones keeping ourselves in stitches, haha. A friend wrote to lament badly paid work because she knew I knew what it was to feel on the periphery, she lamented with a ha, but the ha had fury. Another friend wrote to lament badly paid work because she knew I knew what it was to feel on the periphery, she lamented with beauty, her beauty was regarding the trees, the trees guarding her back, ha.

The sun is shining today, unrepentant. The doctor joked with me when I expressed dismay at being unable to discharge my body on demand in the name of tests. She said she too found it difficult and we laughed. I could feel the sincerity of her care like a tree guarding me. I don't pretend to equate my suffering with yours. I do not want to make an altar of it. Masked into languor, masked into fucking, masked into here, our hunger. Say splendour on our own terms, one friend back home recovering the indigenous place names along the Mississippi, another drawing conversations with the trees to show no still life. So I finally went to the doctor, she regarded me while I moved my bare sack of bones and flesh to try to understand why my lungs kept making a loud rustling sound when I danced.

The body had started to corset around a scarcity of contact. In Germany, if one is insured, one is insured for certain kinds of touch, so she wrote me this Rezept and I was relieved, relieved it was less worse than I thought, there's always some room for transformation, Gott sei Dank, ha. The space between the thoracic vertebrae that had sewed itself shut could become clouds again. A curious, furious beauty. A persistence to show in our dance, every accumulated rage and say, now look: cumulus.

Portemonnaie

to carve out in the empty Platz
a bit of heat grounded and grounding

I had forgotten warmth
in this country where we
were comfortably trying to forget

you ask were asked to put
your uniform back on

it was time for war
it's always time for
war   a war was on

it was not going well
we went on about

the Heizungskosten
as we kept warm
I wanted to find something pliant

in your eyes that fragile blue of
boyhood your boyish wish

to be cruel I admired your resolve
when does money turn to filth swift
and sown of a sow I believed

you better than the ears scattered on
your underheated floor amid the Vuitton

bags hidden beneath the day's groceries
we wanted all the same another sip
of champagne I would want you to protect

me I would want a source of nourishment
not made of ears they are everywhere
we march over them as they detract

from our fun they have been made
into a mountain of rubble upon which

we sit and drink our bubbles we are
on you but cannot see you open
your purse I say open it now

county waste

as a boy I'd watch the worms worm
their way for hours years later my son
did the same : counting them to count
on the continuation of life in death

vivo ma non troppo

I went to hear Patrizia Cavalli read
but she was too sick to travel
from Rome to Berlin
Giorgio Agamben her friend spoke
instead with her Italian - German translator
whose name I forget we are always forgotten
it felt good to be anonymous
vivo ma non troppo
in the dark warm room Agamben said
all poems are either elegies or hymns
and yet Cavalli's poems exist
at the intersection of this Gespräch
which was in Italian what Agamben
actually said was 'l'inno' a word I didn't
know in Italian it sounded to me like 'inner'
I imagined it the key to some bright flame
before we're turned by death   he said
all poems evince change

Neutral Ground

I went down to Saint James infirmary
they had turned it into a planetarium
she was there in the firmament
a constellation to be named
later when we too were dead

what is the use of naming the chaos
scorpion phoenix sea monster lyre crab

where is the place of understanding
as if stage four meant more understanding

advancing

the cava spilled backward

these words another jar

suspended

above the neutral ground
we saw her together

scaling up scaling down from
the stars

How To Survive The Tragedy Of Linear Time

Open up a box to a chorus
of roses. Push the red
button you've been told not to touch.

Let go of worrying over your smart
phone's pulse: un-micro-manage
the macro and look up. The sun

is calling to the trees. The sun is feeding
our wily schemes. Say yes
to coyoted contraptions and no

to every project that requires
a receipt. The sun will sun. The droop
will drop so stop

trying to Tom Cruise your time.
Time has given you what it needs.
The petals: they, too, are singing.

Put a rabbit on it

How close I've come to coming around
        to the flamingo it's like your eyes
how colour can be dietary how far
        from home we become the blue
of the ocean we dove into. If nothing else let's
        be fabulous on the fore of a yacht
or the creek we kayaked through the sexy
        of your mouth because it offers love
though I keep standing pat like a bunny
        ready to run or munch on a carrot
for the crunch.
                Your skin is synecdoche for
        home, even if I forget which part
stands for the whole of the stars
        we crossed. Is it your generosity,
the sun as it gives up on the day
        as you coddle me despite the loud
Romani shouting over the loud seafood?
        Do you doubt my location do you
wish it were fixed the light
        both moves and remains
constant.

hôtel-dieu

In a video essay on Rembrandt's ability to carry the gaze into
another form John Berger talks about accessing the interior of
another person by looking

touching what he calls the hôtel-dieu – a place of disease and
death but also tenderness and love and today I feel happy and
today I say please please me

you do just there in the boyish way you fall when you put on your
shoes – I want to want you that open, untouched by everything
that injures and yet

sometimes I imagine you as a boy, delicate and lost on the streets
of Buenos Aires and then – you take my hand to cross the bridge
back to Berlin

sleeping in a room where we dream and live again

Mercy

I'm facing two stone walruses in a Platz near the death trap,
the death trap a life trap now, there's no one out.

What do walruses dream under a socialist – now
capitalist – regime? I teem with desire. Teem.

Learn the etymology of the verb once meant
to birth, curious, because this morning I woke
to my hands on my bare womb.

Now fertile, I presume, even if any child I'd bear at thirty-seven
would be termed, in the current parlance, a geriatric occurrence.

There is a resurgence. Yesterday
I faced a man I wanted to hold
inside me. Yet we are responsible

citizens – we were social
distancing – texting each other
to avoid saying what we mean.

The cherry blossoms are coming in,
tentative, clean.

space between spaces

my mouth on your mouth then yours then yours

Coming Attraction

Possibilities have always been preferred over endings
it is a question of entry into feeling contained before
it becomes silent

You called three times and it was over
it was ended we played our versions of our movie
in our heads for it was over it was

Then that I called you and my voice was sent to yours
from across great distances a transmission you listened you spoke
into a device that was closer to you than I was this is sometimes
a metaphor and this time it was

Shitty I feel shitty you say and I do too
is also sometimes how you feel after seeing certain movies
you want that part of your life back although you can't have it
back you had gone to see it because you had liked the preview
but not the movie it was awful this is sometimes
not a metaphor for anything it was

Then that you told me when I received your voice
in the receiver that you'd had a movie in your mind that morning
about a time when your mother was doing the dishes and
you were small you wanted to tell her something and
you were going to let your voice be received but
then you noticed her leaning over the kitchen sink crying
lost in the reverberation of her own private movie and
then you knew something that you hadn't before

And that was

Please

Blue is blue because the moon won't give up
its impossible distance

she wants to hold the moon in her mouth
you can dine on it for days

we scampered through a forest
overtaken by mulberries, meaning
we could see – sometimes you feel

like a mother to nobody –

pick the berries
they provide sustenance
substance
a stain that won't quit

home, a long, long way –
you're always going to exist
to some degree through what you do

and don't miss, those hands,
this face, that mouth,
you wish – we missed the moment when

we woke so
our bodies could hello –

it's good to be reminded
of the good kind of impossible

but it's not enough

Blue
is it

HAVE IT

Lundi Gras Lear

A few years ago in New Orleans they made a rule
mandating the safe distance at which ladders must be placed
from the actual parade, and there's been talk of banning them
outright, but then what would the fathers do.

In the Eighties our fathers fashioned purple, green, and gold
spray-painted wooden boxes on ladders for the kids to sit in
and watch the proceedings safely, like a carnival car seat.

I don't get how they learned how to do this
before the advent of the internet,
but it was always the fathers
who would stand behind the children

on the ladders, grounding them with their weight, keeping them
from keening forward if they reached too far
for a painted coconut or a toy dog.

Ours would try to catch whatever beads we couldn't
before they smacked us in the face. For the most part,
he succeeded, though I haven't seen him in years,
and his hands are no longer extended, still I'd like to know him

as a man who'd reach his arms out when needed, still it's hard to
get why he threw his fear in our faces when we were least ready
to catch it, when today is Lundi Gras

and I'm in Arkansas, taking cover from the snow,
when never, never, never, never, never it stings.

You asked me

Comfort is important whether we remember it or not they say children never appreciate their parents enough they are right. We never forget the right things we write about petty grudges but never petty joys. Let there be more petty joys. I wanted to write something for you or right something for you because Mother's Day. Perhaps it is crazy to name certain feelings which is why I am writing around the naming maybe writing over feeling. I want to name things without reaching for poetic reaching because lately I dislike language in poetry poets write thinking it sounds right poetic – cicadas latin epigrams and professors professing death from summer rentals in France – but here I am trying to write you a poem for you I am trying your patience I am trying isn't that what children always do.

thermodynamics

Saturday night in Glasgow,
        along the snow-packed sidewalks
needled voices say, Please,
        say, I know what I'm doing, say, Ma'am,
say something sweet. Why do I doubt
        the good, insist
on shaking my fist
        after the bad. Some dumb self-
punishing mechanism.
        I'm trying to be better at
forgiveness, that little floe
        forged in the centre of the Kelvin
determined not to melt;
        I admire its stubbornness,
tire of the familiar
        refusal to surrender all.
Stefi, when you opened your hands,
        let them alight on my head,
the passerine trapped in the chest
        where more might give gave flight.

I promise to be good

if the MRI says the houseguest in her brain

is malevolent the chance of survival is

grim I want to hold her hand and invite

the guest in somewhere else not here not

this her smile always carries the promise

that life will be more beautiful or painful

look at the old glory of Naples this her

home the city a tumour that wants to be

light when it is finished with the dark

512 hours
Marina Abramović, London

The Serpentine walk we were led down led us to expect
redemption in the form of art. We got there and I lay down,

defeated; you walked around. People were enacting their ideas
about being watched; they wanted to be;

you were weary because they kept telling you
what to do – a flaw in the texture of the artwork,

a flaw in the texture of life itself – while I wanted to lie there
all afternoon. When was the last time you were in a room,

sleeping, and there was light left in the day, and
twenty-some-odd people? Heads down, there was

nothing left to perform except the good will
in that drawn space, which we attuned

through the white of our noise-cancelling headphones –

Consecration: The Superbowl Edition

My students said they spoke about the Saints on the Spanish news but I don't have a TV so I couldn't tell you. I remember as a girl watching them lose while we prayed for intercession of a different kind. In Madrid I am far away from the divine and so the win seems like another story, which it is, good news. The Sky News announcer forgot to mention that it's almost Mardi Gras. It's an open question whether we will make it to the sky, which is what the Spanish call heaven, or if what awaits us is something like the end of Carnival in New Orleans, this year the 17th of February at 0.00 hours, Ash Wednesday: absence the only volume in the Quarter, the street sweepers brushing the sidewalks clean.

a sum which is less than the whole of its parts

a stolen conversation

I've never met anyone who died before.
El mudo no hablaba inglés.
The top of my heart can't communicate with the bottom.
And this.

Bartleby & Co.

I believe fiction is the only thing
that brings me closer
to the truth that

                Reality obscures

Not long ago

                I dreamed of a poem
                written as though it belonged
                to the place where I am

John Ashbery said in my book:

                "Having lived in Paris
                unfits you for living anywhere,
                including Paris"

My greatest virtue is being
one of the few honest people
in my life that I've known

                This thought,
                the product of anxiety,
                only comes to me
                in the evenings

Lavapiés

She lived in an attic on protection street in the barrio washfeet
which she forgot to do sometimes the hot water running over her
back in the cold apartment, her hair was greying she thought
but it was just her ánimo that turned and okay a stray hair or two
but her back was still young, the clouds swam by and
the full moon did its full-on thing through the attic skylight.
At times she'd wake to dry air or the sound of a dog barking,
cold because she couldn't afford the heat.

as long as we are here
Antigone Sr./Twenty Looks or Paris Is Burning at the Judson Church (L),
Santiago

We are el chico en la fila B

we are going to dance

by watching our work

track forward from Pinochet

SIDA Cassandra's scream

we are every neuron

in Rob Fordeyn's

cocky swing we are

mothers to each other

in one fierce dream we

are going from Harlem

to Paris in Santiago

de Chile we are not

going to stop coming

home a matter of vindication

for every man who couldn't

get up and say

this is who I am

this is what we are

If you are local, please bring your own lawnchairs

Today my friend Denise emailed me from Guayaquil to say her ex-boyfriend had a website; this website had to do with the most tropical name; a bad translation; there were dollars and Hitlers but no Usnavys (read: Oos-*nah*-bees).

Today the New York Times condescended to name duck hunters in Louisiana; I wanted to care, but didn't; sometimes we only know what we condescend to read; sometimes it falls from the air like nerve gas like anything; a feeling: Assad: concern: abstracted: a visit to the Style section.

They were asked by the guns	
to kneel and give up:	*What* – their phones
To be happy is to put such things:	*Where* – out of your mind
To be happy is to accept them:	*How* – { }
To be what hasn't happened:	*When* – not to you not yet
To be:	*Why* – the privilege-vent

Big Easy Anthropology

[*medium*]
if you are a woman of a certain means
you can learn how to be nonthreatening
by visiting anthropologie.com or
the frou frou store in Canal Place

I do not pay full price for my ruffles
I do not get paid to look this good
because I am not worth it not
like the girl on the website

who went to my middle school
her mother was my gym teacher
in grammar school she would have us
do an exercise called washing machine

she would yell at me because
I would do it wrong or stop
now women now stop
doing that with your hands

it isn't that it's this
the boys did it too
hands on hips now twist but
what are the athletic benefits

maybe in the obliques they are less
threatening than the rectus abdominis
now go to a barre class and become
more threatening by getting smaller

[*large*]
there is Rebecca leaning on a fleur-de-lis gate Uptown
because we New Orleans ladies do this in our spare time
though she and I both grew up in the same ugly suburb
where the ducks in the canals have red cancerous necks

and look older than Old [sic] Metairie the oldest suburb
in the city unless you count Uptown which you should
because that's where the Americans lived which is what
the Creoles in the Quarter called the Colonial arrivistes

who built Corinthian columns with their cottoned money
flourishes meant to legitimize their Kardashian newness
but now the sliver by the river is where old white money
live it didn't flood because the old new money knew to

settle on naturally high ground that Katrina could not drown
and now New Yorkers buy houses on the other side of town
above St. Claude they call it Bywater even though it's not
the city a marketing tool for cool for interesting for Rebirth

I saw a brass band code for *I see black people* code for
the city whiter and more segregated now code for *safer*
code among certain whites for *less black* said sotto voce
it is better or worse than white girls like my friend and

I created the Kool Kats Klub in 1988 not thinking
of the konnotation to spell it like that the year the grand wizard
David Duke tried to run for president and again in '92
he didn't win when Anthro Rebecca and I were ten

46

[*small*]
she looked the same then as she does at 32
she is painting birds on my poem like tendrils and
we call ourselves artists and say we like nature and
we sure could use some clothes from Anthropologie

spare me $300 to feel pretty I own three dresses
from the store but one I don't wear much
I worry it's too 'Kim K'/too tight in the butt
and one is too dressy but the other I love

so please just study your sociologie
and remember if you are a woman
you may want to end with :) or !
if you are a man please don't :)

thanks so much I appreciate it!

Rinascimaiale

A wonderful Sicilian mechanic from
   another century told me that it's easier
to regulate the pressure in your cannoli
   than it is in your knuckled soul.

Avoid falling
   in love with bureaucracy –
I'm not, I'm not, I promised –

   I'd just like to ask you
to do the laundry again.
   Curiosity is a tide

made visible by the female
   hands drawing nonsense
yours are reluctant

   to enact. Too bad.
The pig is already dead.

Please

Dear holy mothers everywhere
do you know how many bros
go to Düsseldorf just to say no

to saying no and today

my diagonal ache angles the quiet
man at the window on the train
for a sideways hit that
we might not survive today and

standing on the mountaintop screaming
for help isn't necessary for holy mothers
everywhere we
have phones
we can call and we
are
so small

We are happy on the isola are you are you

the nuns are waving hello across   the river's
mouth   he cottoned   to her smell
a bath was drawn   stupid lady   parts curtsy
for every war   the choir boys in the zeppelin   sing
I forgot the latin gotta go with your pinafored waiting
wait   where was it   I wanted   to be   a child
waiting   on the plain   aflame   weeping lost
in the nightclub rain   it rains   we did nothing
to distil our dread   the dead   ain't afraid of
nobody   they   believing nothing
since the day they   wasn't   born
my mouth   you never   warned me
warm me   love   the nuns   wave hello
I offer you my neck   the little lambkins   bleat
please me   will you   answer their call

Please

A woman once consoled me by offering nothing
other than her presence we all want

so abject I thought if I followed my mother's dictum to fast
I would get closer to her holy mother dear god I felt no god

at the Popeye's on 23rd and 8th in Manhattan I ate a biscuit
last week my madeleine moment for Lent

to repent aged twelve or thirteen I would eat one two max three
biscuits from the franchise a day my Metairie bread and water

fasting we were chosen we had chosen to get pure
I would get there through my hunger I wanted

to be whole make me whole again please
some pleasure carried forth and piped in from Basin Street

ALL

Fun fact

In certain cultures the future
to the back where we can't see
than we can the weather

dreams have been worse
the content I think of Gregor
dreams it depends on
ease back out of my body
up and wake less certain

I never study the forecast
I guess I like to be surprised
disappointment the problem
to everything unlikely or fantastic
disappointed or maybe a bit slow

I never saw it coming the car
of an accident and
from Sex and the City
in an episode from
was performing
three hundred feet away
hold a magic wand and
differently what

what is it you think
something hopeful

is referred to with a gesture
because we can't predict the future anymore
though there are portents I know my anxiety

than usual lately though I don't remember
Samsa and his 'troubled' or 'uneasy'
how it's translated I want to translate my dis-
or tell it to shut the fuck
of all that I'm uncertain about

the prevision as it's called in Romance languages
not to worry to look forward not back not risk
as I see it is that I am good at looking forward
as I am idealistic meaning I am constantly
to adapt to life's crutches and time's arrow for

when it hit that's the whole point
I didn't expect to see an actress in a scene
manhandling a vibrator in a Sharper Image
fifteen years ago the same actress who
at that same moment in a play called *Look Away*
from where I watch her past self incredulous
I bet she thought it would all go down
actress doesn't want to be famous and

she sees in her previsions now
I hope

available memory

There is a message on the back of her hand,
a place she should know better, he says

a woman is turning away from
a man turning away from a woman

according to the history of sex,
Lacan said love was an exchange

of projections by the strapped, but surely
there's more to it than that,

to love or to the quote, you ask, if
improvisation is a means of keeping

the *sospiro* suspended,
what thrums inside us

should not be mended
for to do so is to give up

the possibility of our happy
sadness, to sit inside the *yet*

is to admit she wants to have
more to do less, while on the curve

where the head of the femur bone
inserts beneath the pelvic crest,

he kissed, to elicit not love or respect,
but bliss, her own, or his, whatever natural

disaster was contained
in all this, she does not regret

what's left –
she's making space for it.

Please

St. Joe's altars in New Orleans have a pile of abundance
that's been sitting out for too long it's best not
to eat it I wonder what to do with my anger
when it's been sitting out for too long I feel full
from love today a kind of trinitarian Liebe I woke up
startled from a dream that a man I had
loved loved me and wrote the word three times in an email:
Liebe. Liebe. Liebe.
I never got the email.
He sent it to an address I had for fifteen odd years
an account that a spambot attacked and I deleted and
is now owned by someone in Crimea who may or may not
pretend to be me one day but isn't fun fact: if you get an email
from xxxxxxxxxx@yahoo.com even though for years it was me
it's not fun fact: if you send an email to xxxxxxxxxx@yahoo.com
even though for years I would read it I won't I can't.
In the dream the man I had loved was telling my sister
that he wanted to commit
to some one some thing. He was married. Dear Reader
to be honest I don't know if he truly loved me he told me once
the word Liebe is so much stronger
than what we mean in English by love
but then he said in his way that he loved me and I'd like
to think he did. I did. Love him and finally
am no longer ashamed by the spear that pierced
my flesh
did not ask but was given

Dear Jesus

It's nothing personal, but
the cardinal perched on the sign
outside my apartment complex
makes me almost not sad
about the April Fool's wedding

I didn't attend. Understand,
my favourite part of Mass
when I was still young
enough to be forced to attend
was when you'd turn around

and shake my hand. And also
with you I went two or three
times to the Polish church
in Greenpoint during the half-
second I lived on N. 9th and Wythe

because the gold communion-
catchers and the crowd of young
people reciting a language I didn't
speak was the trip I wanted but couldn't
take because I worked six days a week.

Understand, when my mother
says to trust in you I mostly
feel resentful, then resentful
of that resentment. I've spent a half-
life trying to get around to trusting

the glut of revelations that come
from the scintilla animating us –
and wouldn't you know, philosophers
still haven't solved the puzzle
of all-too-human consciousness.

In the catechism toy box hide
Catholic Guilt cuddly bear, Lapsed
Catholic dolly, Bastardized Catholic
action figure and Recovering Catholic
playing cards, which nobody purchased

at my garage sale. Understand,
they were only a quarter each,
but people have too much stuff
as it is. And maybe they didn't know
the secrets you confess to me

at every service I miss. Dear Jesus,
don't worry, I won't tell anyone,
I know how hard it is to believe.
If it helps, you can have that
heavylight box for free.

the sounds you make when embarrassed but saying thank you

She starts spazzing out over the usual broken eggs –
her eye on how many are left in the carton, as always.

So you text her: at the end of the day you've got folks in your life
who aren't gonna let bad things happen to you, remember this;

and all she can feel is grateful to have a friend who
seems to see right past her issues with breakfast.

In the waiting room, we hedge every desire
with four edges and inflate it, swaying

in time to the silver clouds overhead, though
we have to punch them periodically in order

to keep them aloft: our whimsy takes effort:
is that part of the problem, or the solution;

that depends; if your uterus is older than thirty
being asked to fill in *Yes / No / Never / Unsure*

is liable to bring up _____
because doctors are nosy, like your friends

who sing Stretch Marks in the same key
Gilda Radner did, and laugh, because

our poems aren't/are children, without the residual medical expenses.

Warhol's only venture into set design
were those mylar *Clouds* I mentioned,

and after he was shot he began carrying precious
gems in his pockets: rubies, diamonds, emeralds:

the egg/carton problem all over again; as Billy
Name once said: Andy just wanted to make

the world safe for Andy; and I think how
your friendship makes the world safer

for so many of us, and I hope you'll accept
these modest noises in acknowledgment.

You Can Have It All

I've been listening to George McCrae sing on
repeat sometimes the breeze of want is enough, my feet,
caressed by a man I barely know and maybe won't never

ever ever ever. We would like to thank the concerned parties
for their concerned partying. The guillotine was a gag, promise,
though practice what you will beneath the foam blade if

you insist on showing off. In the glass box, the billionairess
sat in silk, smiling, we perfected our torches in the mirror
feeling good about ourselves. It was not my bent

to burn your what I meant to reflect on this time,
the bonsai we agreed on pruning. It'll be perfect
tomorrow. That's what the shears are for. You

You do you

On the bayou there's no one to sing to but the birds it is for them you feel sometimes a song in yourself pushing against your mind from your mouth and asking you to expand the movement but it is less elegant and less likely than the egret's flight. Your favourite thing is to watch them take off, a light in your room and the sun going down behind the water. The window overlooks the Terrebonne bayou and there are also herons and ducks and gulls and pelicans and the occasional hawk and grackles and vultures, too. There are no people in your world nor in theirs. They are avoided by taking to the sky. In the good earth behind the double-wide yellow weeds don't bloom so much as take over, suddenly and without warning.

Kegger in Georgi Balanchivadze's Backyard

Black bile, yellow bile, blood, phlegm:
we pledged – to divide ourselves up
and played flip cup to determine
who'd bust a move to begin.

Best not to let the big muscle
groups take over in classical
training they must be tempered
by the slow-twitch fibres to

support the most natural leaps
to conclusion. Dance teachers love
to talk about the magic of muscle
memory, the notion that, you do it

often enough, the nerves do
the remembering for you, but
that was also Mr. B.'s gloss on
the dissemination of sorostitutes.

We gave the garden gnomes
our neon shirts to better wave
our legs in the air, petit-allegro-style
giddy even though the sanguine gals

don't menstruate – it's all good,
for the man says it keeps us quick
on our backs. Is it wrong that we're happy
to oblige him? Have you seen the majesty

of the extended line ~~on~~ in the mirror?
We commit to it because giving in
to the Russian's unnatural demands gives us
our regular transubstantiation of *Hoc est corpus*.

Two Cut Short

IN THE INVISIBLE HIERARCHY of artists, dancers are at the top, because dance is the least egocentric of all art forms, because dancers give themselves to an art that betrays them as they occupy: space: time: the body. Then musicians, particularly those who sit in the orchestra pit, who are less visible but also less cheated by time. Then painters. Then architects, who can be infantile, and sometimes have a messiah complex. It depends. Then actors – and rock stars, who are actors of a kind – for they are dependably transparent in their need. But writers, writers are at the bottom, for they want everything and pretend to want nothing, and delude themselves with the idea that their art will redeem them beyond what they occupy: space: time: the body.   So: writers are at the bottom. Writers are the worst.

AFTER THE THIRD DAY in the five-star hotel we had grown accustomed to the affluence around us, and became resentful when our room wasn't cleaned a second time that day, as promised. We felt we were owed something, and the women who cleaned up after us felt they were owed something, too. We were careful not to imagine them though their names were written on tiny cards with each day's forecast. We enjoyed the pretence of our luxury, and wanted to remain inside it while we could.

A Brief History of Art & Commerce
[Met edition, NY]

       at a moneyed tomb
a woman offers me a cookie
       in exchange for
ideas
       I refuse the cookie
and offer up
       my thoughts
for free
       she keeps
asking me why
       I refuse to eat
in the museum
       she wants to know
where am I going later
       with my friends
I don't know
       I tell her but
I do know
       I just don't want
to tell her
       for marketing purposes
       and
an hour
       later
I'm hungry
       and notice
       a cookie
       in the museum
costs four dollars and seventy-five cents before tax
       suddenly

I regret
I didn't say yes
to the cookie

the grammarians

the cows were wandering
through a meadow
a meadow not a pasture
they had refused to eat
they were refusing
because they felt far from life
even though they
wouldn't have articulated it as such
after all, they're just cows

small creatures collectively

the deer gathered outside my window
surrender their white tails
I remember once in Arkansas
a large buck was trapped
near the creek and couldn't get free
it leapt in vain into a chain link fence I
felt its distress and was powerless
to help it
in marameo a large dance studio
in the centre of Berlin I listened to Edwin
a former dancer for Birmingham Royal Ballet
say take a picture
if we could get the balance right
we'd be free
that was the idea
I loved ballet
for its im-possibilities for
the invitation to fail so
beautifully

less like an object and more like the weather

Let's leave the pliés and spinal curves and attitudes out of it,
unless they serve to keep our bodies warm. Cunningham said
dance *gives you nothing back ... no paintings ... no poems ... nothing*
but that single fleeting moment when you feel alive.

I could feel the weight of my bones gather what was left
of the waxed floor and find in the fascia a quiet joyous potential,
alive to the impish capacity of our joints to do
what we don't expect to our gratitude. Surprise yourself

if you can at least once a week, find a way to get from *a* to *b*
without using your fore or hind limbs, or from *b* to *a*
using only your memories. Merce was waiting for me there
on the platform, the local had switched to express

and told no one, so I told him about the time I saw five dancers
push at the limit of what moving meant: one dancer
giving up a backward curve so generous
her lambent head nearly emptied of logic.

pas de don't

no

no   step should be codified

of a barre   you can

it will leave you

grew up asked

et al   embody

embrace the ability

rehearse every

abandon it

searching for

though I could I do enjoy

hold on and know

reverent dancers

to bow   before

obligation like ex-

to fail   at what

doubt 'til   it's

altogether a little

a second

the solemn certitude

once you're warm

I know who

Bournonville

altar boys do we

we know

perfected   or else

lighter   still

longer—

For love only

everybody was given permission
that was the most beautiful thing about it

obsessed with a serious exaggeration unlikely I thought
I'd let you go
offstage after your performance the dancers
were working with the fragility
of urgency the urgent fragility of our shared subjects

weather and time
those little shifts to be caught
and kissed because
the movement of life is the only thing

you said as one dancer fell forward and another cowered
before a cow's head and the grass asserted itself
through the sidewalk reasons for leaping

and keeping in mind what Trisha said
after the puppies were born you know
civilization has continued

and it's best
to be less precious about
art is an act of generosity

I thought as I stood in the cold brick chapel as
the director explained the money people said it should be sold
but it's still there as you are and
that was the most beautiful thing

Please

The Benedictines benedictate
a stillness I keep trying to refresh, opening
a new window and another and another,
minimizing tongues I can't seem to understand.
The more I acquire the less I inhabit any one well.
On the trail small ceramics of Jesus invoke
death, compassion, guilt, sin, death,
compassion, love. Misery is a modality
a fault line I fall into time to time,
at the place where felled trees sleep
next to hungry sheep. When I saw them,
the bells clanging too many chords,
all at once, scared, scared of, scared off,
we turned, wayward, home.

Notes

"Put a rabbit on it": in French '*de poser un lapin*' is an idiom meaning 'to stand someone up'. According to the Oxford American Dictionary, the origins of the word 'coddle' may be 'a dialect variant of the obsolete *caudle* [administer invalids' gruel].'

Marina Abramović's *512 Hours* was held in the Serpentine Gallery in June 2014; the phrase 'flaw[s] in the texture of life itself' is from Mary Gaitskill, which she borrowed from Nabokov.

"Bartleby & Co." takes its title from the novel by Enrique Vila-Matas and is composed entirely of text from interviews with the author in English and Spanish.

"as long as we are here" is dedicated to the man in row B, seat 6 at the Jan 8, 2014 performance of Trajal Harrell's *Antigone Sr.* [...] at the GAM in Santiago, Chile.

The title "the sounds you make when [you're] embarrassed but saying thank you" and the phrase 'modest noises' are from Andy Warhol and Pat Hackett's book *POPism*; Warhol's *Silver Clouds*, first exhibited in Leo Castelli's gallery in 1966, were then commissioned by Merce Cunningham for his company's 1968 piece *RainForest*; because the Clouds were unpredictable in their movements, some were tethered to the ground for later performances. Gilda Radner sang "Stretch Marks" as Patti Caldwell in an SNL sketch from 1980. The poem is for Diana.

"Kegger in Georgi Balanchivadze's backyard": George Balanchine choreographed *The Four Temperaments* in 1946 for what later became New York City Ballet.

"Two Cut Short" are inspired by Umberto Saba's *Scorciatoie* [Shortcuts].

"less like an object and more like the weather" is how John Cage described the dances of his partner and collaborator Merce Cunningham.

"pas de don't": August Bournonville was a Romantic choreographer noted for refining the use of gesture in classical dance; his legacy survives in the subtle elegance of the Royal Danish Ballet.

"For love only": this poem was written with the kind support of a Robert Rauschenberg Foundation Archives Research Residency, the title and quote in italics are Rauschenberg's; sincere thanks to Francine, Shirin, and everyone at the foundation.

Acknowledgments

Thanks to Alessio, David, Diana, Elisa, Ipek, Jeffrey, Jörg, Margaret, Vickie and Al, for their warm friendship; to Art Omi, where some of these poems were revised; to Davis, Geoff, and Geffrey of the University of Arkansas MFA program for their thoughts on an early draft of this book; to the editors and staff of the publications where some of the poems first appeared: *Barrow Street*, *berlin lit*, *The Best American Poetry* blog, *Blackbird*, *The Cincinnati Review*, *Colorado Review*, *The Common*, *Diagram*, *diode*, *Electric Literature*, *elimae*, *Fence*, *Forklift, Ohio*, *jubilat*, *Make*, *Map Literary*, *map – Media / Archive / Performance*, *The New Yorker*, *Pank*, *Salamander*, *Sixth Finch*, *Sonora Review*, and *Witness*; and to Susan, Hugh, and Nastassja of MOIST, *grazie di tutto*.

About the Author

Kathleen Heil is a writer/translator and choreographer/performer whose poetry, fiction, and translations appear in *The New Yorker*, *The Common*, *The Stinging Fly*, *The Paris Review*, and other journals. She is also the translator of *The Loveliest Vowel Empties*, Meret Oppenheim's collected poems, and of *Sophie Taeuber-Arp's Letters to Annie and Oskar Müller-Widmann*. Born and raised in New Orleans, she presently resides in Berlin.

YOU CAN HAVE IT ALL is the second book in MOIST's fourth season.